INDIAN CULTURE

By

Holly Duhig

©2017
Book Life
King's Lynn
Norfolk PE30 4LS

ISBN: 978-1-78637-199-7

Written by:
Holly Duhig

Edited by:
Charlie Ogden

Designed by:
Evie Wright

A catalogue record for this book
is available from the British Library

PHOTO CREDITS

Abbreviations: l-left, r-right, b-bottom,
t-top, c-centre, m-middle.

Front cover – LuckyImages. 2 – Sean Hsu. 3 – szefei. 4 – Alexandra Lande. 5tl – Alex
Hubenov. 5tm – v.s.anandhakrishna. 5tr – rawmn. 5cl – Shyamalamuralinath. 5cl –
Katrina Elena. 5cr – SNEHIT. 5bl – kudla. 5bm – imagedb.com. 5br – singh_lens.
6 – Daniel Prudek. 7l – Mikadun. 7r – Girish Menon. 8 – Tukaram.Karve.
9 – Dana Ward. 10 – Olena Tur. 11 – Mario Boutin. 12 – Filip Fuxa. 13 – szefei. 14tl –
sunsetman. 14tr – Casper1774 Studio. 14bl – Dmitry Rukhlenko. 14br – saiko3p. 15l
– saiko3p. 15r – Dipak Shelare. 16 – Dragon Images. 17 – CRS PHOTO. 18 – Curioso. 19
– Alexandra Lande. 20 – India Picture. 21 – Swapnil A P. 22l – Christian Bertrand. 22r –
GlebStock. 23l – AdaCo. 23r – Dima Sobko.

Images are courtesy of Shutterstock.com.
With thanks to Getty Images,
Thinkstock Photo and iStockphoto.

CONTENTS

Words that look like **this** can be found in the glossary on page 24.

WHAT IS CULTURE?

A culture is the beliefs and ideas of a group of people. For many people, culture is very important.

Food

History

Traditions

Many things go into making a culture.

Religion

Location

Communities

WHAT MAKES A CULTURE?

Clothes

Family

Art

WHERE IS INDIA?

China

Pakistan

The Himalayas

India

Nepal

India is bordered by Pakistan, China and Nepal. The Himalayan mountain range also stretches across the north of India.

NEW DELHI

FACT:

A street in New Delhi called Khari Baoli is home to the biggest spice market in Asia.

New Delhi, India

India has a **population** of over 1.3 billion people. India's capital city is New Delhi.

COMMUNITIES

Salunkwadi, India

Groups of people that live in the same area are called communities. People in the same community often share the same culture. In Salunkwadi, life is focused around farming.

India also has many big communities called cities. In New Delhi, life is very busy and there are many people and cars rushing about.

New Delhi, India

9

LANDMARKS

Taj Mahal, India

Landmarks often have a lot of history, which can make them important to a culture. The Taj Mahal is a famous landmark in India. It is a **mausoleum** that was built for an ancient king's beloved wife.

The River Ganges flows through India. It is an important landmark in Indian culture and many people in India believe its water is **sacred**.

The Ganges

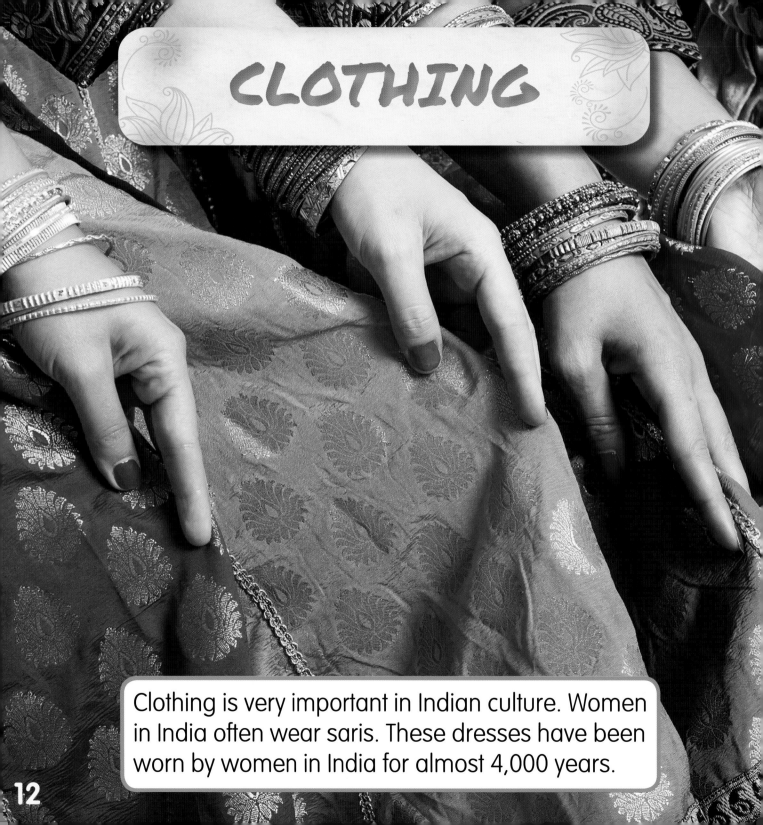

CLOTHING

Clothing is very important in Indian culture. Women in India often wear saris. These dresses have been worn by women in India for almost 4,000 years.

There are over 80 different ways to wear a sari. The number and direction of **pleats** in a woman's sari can be used to show her religious beliefs.

RELIGION

Hindu temple

Buddhist temple

Sikh temple

Jain temple

Four important religions – Hinduism, Buddhism, Sikhism and Jainism – all began in India. The most popular religion in India is Hinduism.

One important Hindu **festival** is Diwali. Diwali is known as 'the festival of lights'. Diwali has been celebrated in India for thousands of years.

FACT:

People light diya lamps like these during Diwali festival.

LANGUAGE

Many people believe the language they speak is important to their culture. There are over 22 languages spoken in India. The most popular language is Hindi.

People in the same community often speak the same language. Many languages in India are **endangered** because they are only spoken by a few communities.

FOOD

Food can be a big part of a person's culture. Indian food is known for using many colourful spices.

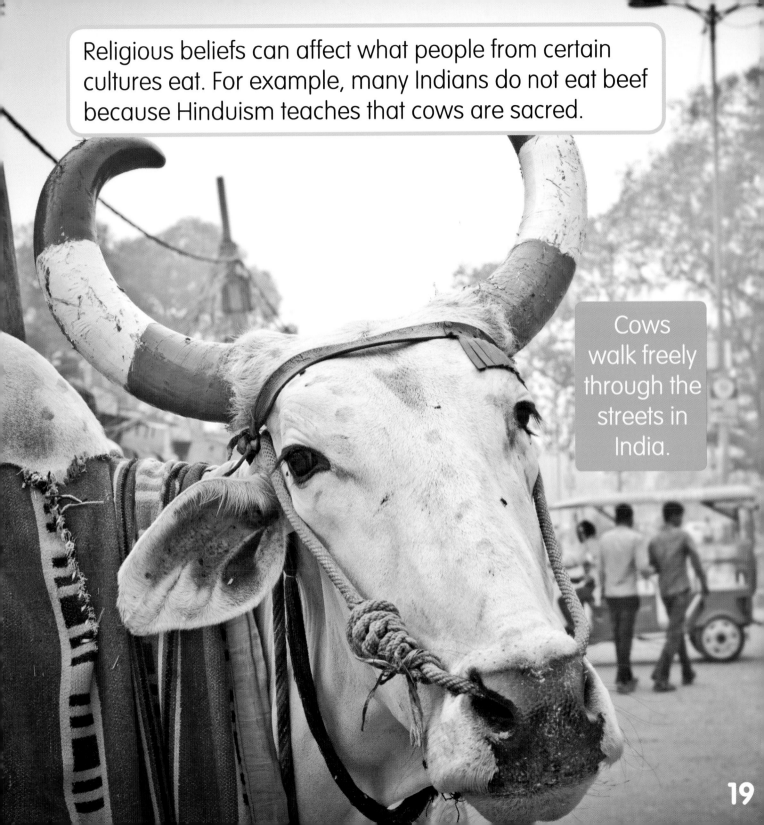

Religious beliefs can affect what people from certain cultures eat. For example, many Indians do not eat beef because Hinduism teaches that cows are sacred.

Cows walk freely through the streets in India.

19

AT HOME

Indian family celebrating a birthday

Family is very important in Indian culture. Many children live with their aunts, uncles and grandparents as well as their parents.

Weddings are very important in Indian culture. The family and friends of the couple getting married come together to celebrate.

FUN FACTS

India is famous for its Hindi-language films. These films are known as Bollywood films.

Yoga began in India.

For special events, women in India often decorate their skin with henna tattoos.

Chess was first played India.

GLOSSARY

festival	a time when people come together and celebrate a special event
landmarks	places or buildings that are famous or easily recognised
mausoleum	a building where one or more dead people are buried
pleats	folds in a piece of clothing
population	the number of people living in a place
sacred	connected with a religious belief and deserving of respect

INDEX